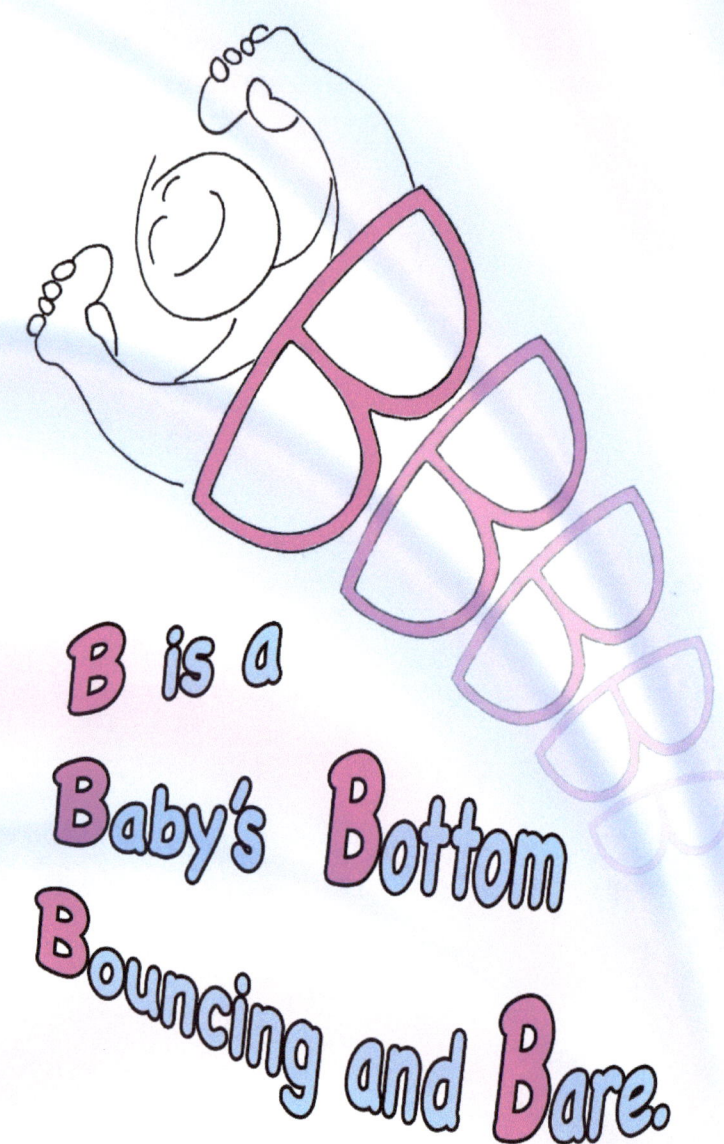

B is a Baby's Bottom Bouncing and Bare.

C, Could be Coughing –

GERMS everywhere.

With E as an Ear, what would you hear?

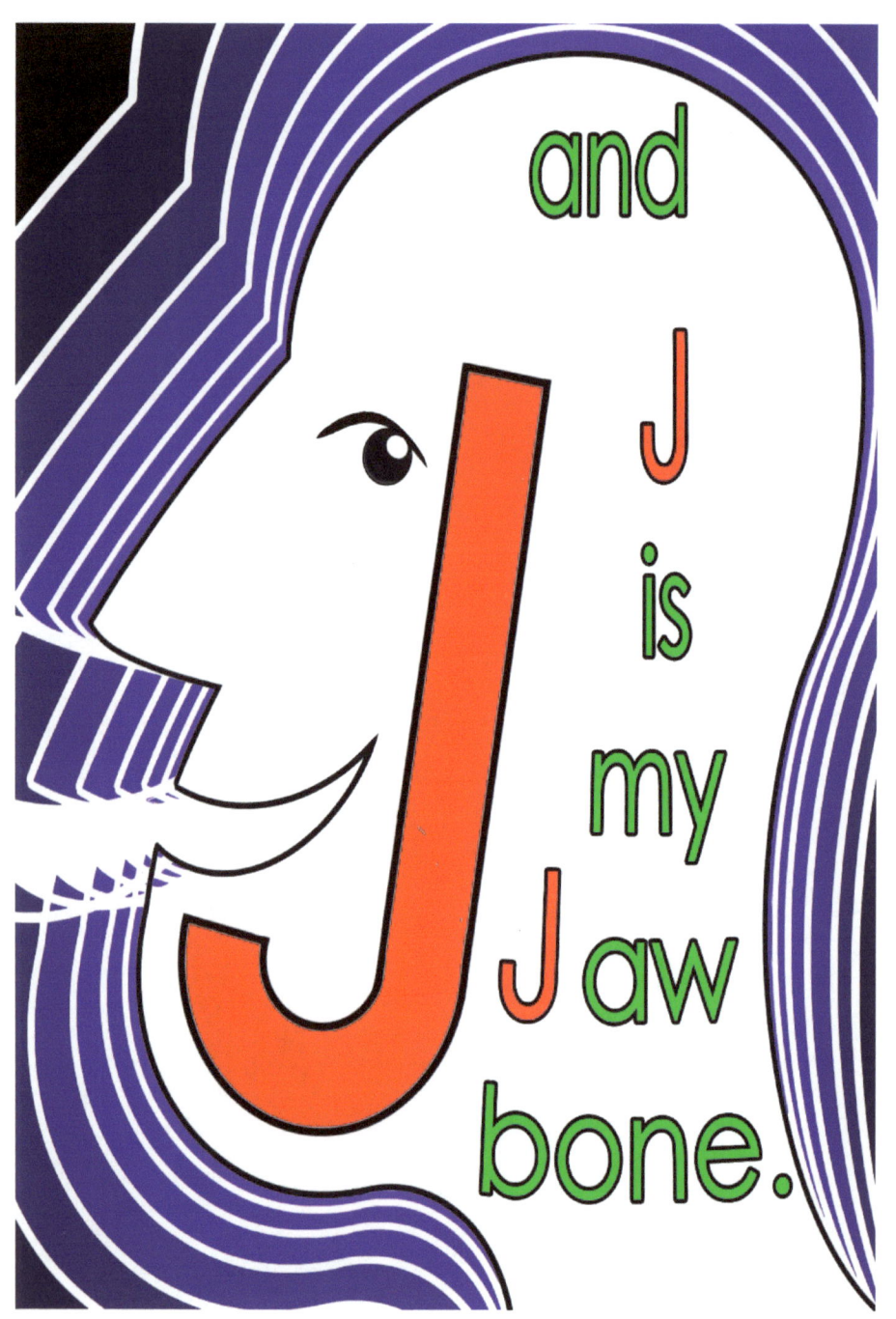

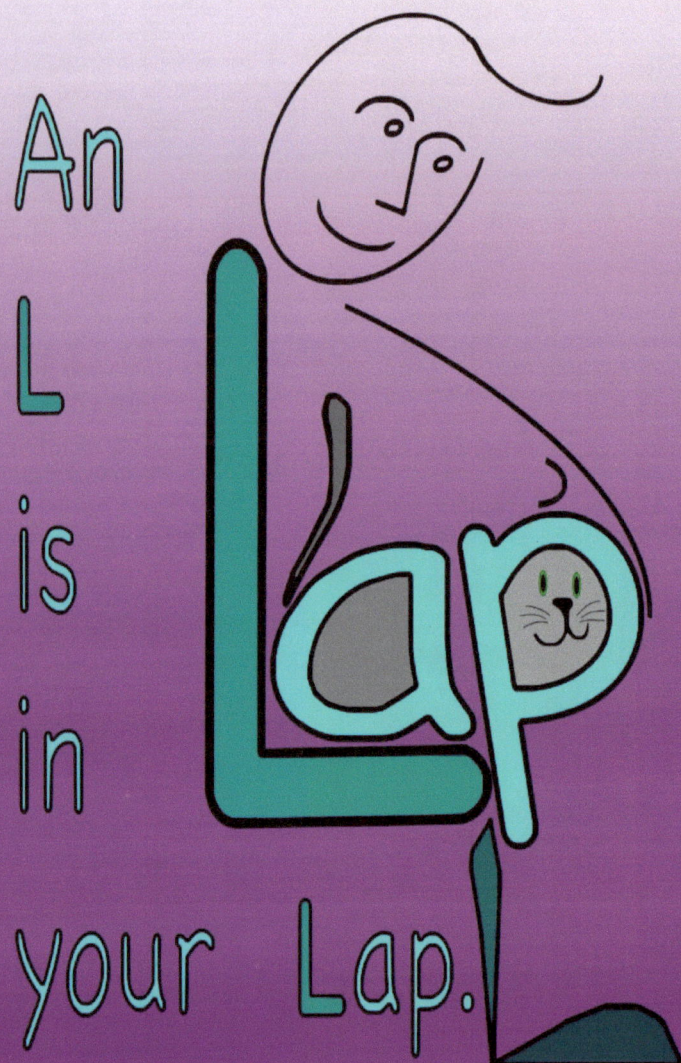

Mighty Mountains, you Might need a Map.

N has been Naughty.

Your face has an O-

and your mouth makes this shape when you say

R is Reaching for one of your toys.

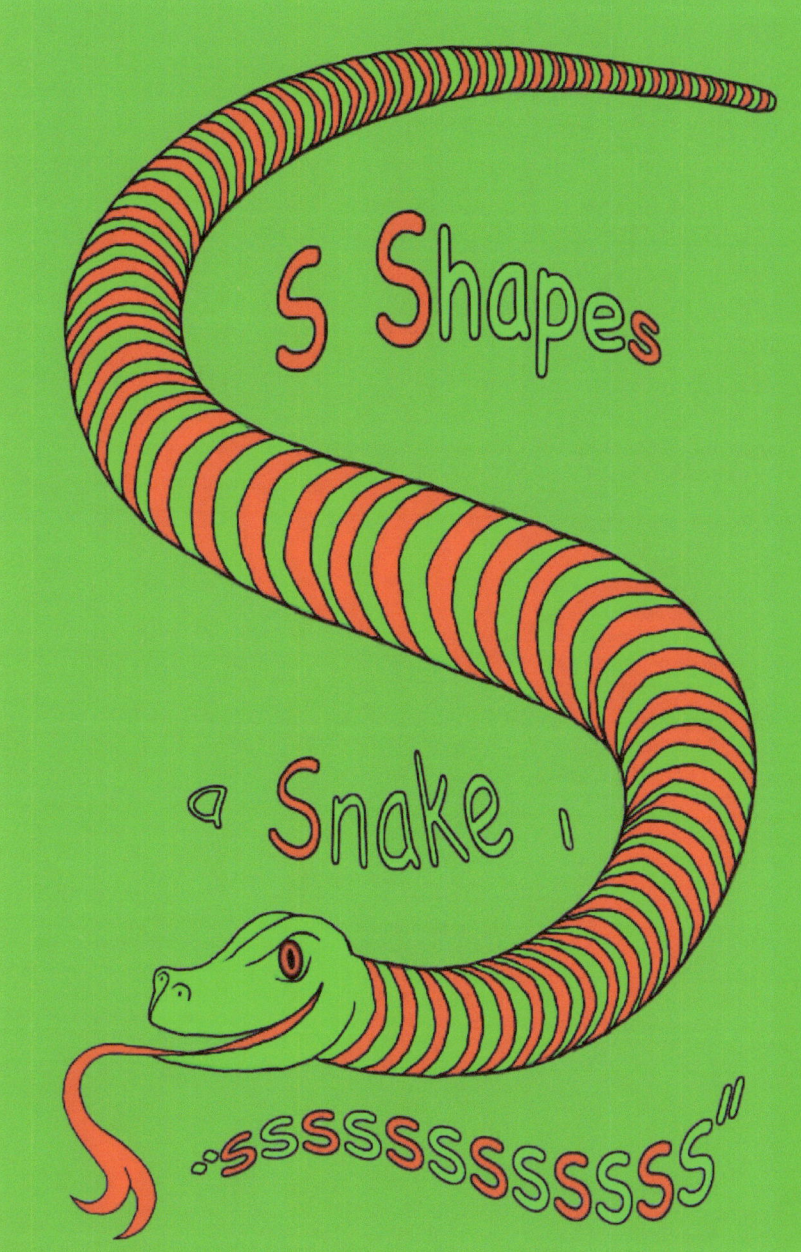

Drink from the U in cup **CUP** if you are able.

X marks the spot.

SLUMP

EEhump

EELEVATOR

Eyes, eyes, eyes.
Look and see.
WOW MOM ME WE

D J Smith is a native of California's San Francisco Bay Area, who as a child had great difficulty learning to read. *"My parents hoped that I would prove to be at least average."* D J has lived in the "City of Angels" for a few decades where he has enjoyed designing, painting and sculpting scenery and props for stage, theme parks, film and television until 2010 when M.S. disabled him. He is now engaged fulltime in front of his MAC, editing video and finally finishing his illustrated stories. *"Life can sure have a strange way of getting you to do something that you really should have been doing all along."*

IMAGINE AN ALPHABET was born out of this father's nightly, after school struggle with his daughter and her homework. *"An obviously intelligent child, she could not make heads or tails out of the printed word. She would declare, "But Daddy, the letters keep jumping all around?!" Eventually she was diagnosed and labeled as being dyslexic and also, not so oddly enough intellectually gifted. With a pervasive "one size fits all" approach, school can be quite challenging for kids like my daughter. People with dyslexia can be exceptional, they must by nature think outside of the box, often improving all of our lives."*

"When looking at the printed page most of us have no problem separating the letters and words on the page from one another. For those with dyslexia and other learning difficulties LETTER IDENTIFACATION can be a huge problem. I started asking my daughter, and myself, what do these 26 letters actually look like? Let's not worry about how they fit into words just yet, but let's just imagine that if these letters were things, real objects, what would they be? We were going to find a new and better way to figure out those pesky letters!"

D J is passionate about igniting in children the desire for education and knowledge. Believing that learning can and should be enjoyable, he is working on a series of books sure to provide plenty more fun with letters, words, and language.

The author dedicates this book to *Xandie*.

www.ingramcontent.com/pod-product-compliance
Lightning Source LLC
Chambersburg PA
CBHW041744040426
42444CB00001B/24